Excel 365
Pivot Tables

EASY EXCEL 365 ESSENTIALS - BOOK 4

M.L. HUMPHREY

CONTENTS

Introduction

This book is part of the *Easy Excel 365 Essentials* series of titles. These are targeted titles that are excerpted from the main *Excel 365 Essentials* series and are focused on one specific topic.

If you want a more general introduction to Excel, then you should check out the *Excel 365 Essentials* titles instead. In this case, *Intermediate Excel 365* which covers pivot tables as well as a number of other topics, such as charts and conditional formatting.

But if all you want is a book that covers this specific topic, then let's continue with a discussion of how to create pivot tables and pivot charts in Microsoft Excel.

(Note that this book does not cover basic charts, just pivot charts, so it assumes that you already have knowledge of charts. If you don't, *Intermediate Excel 365* covers both topics.)

Pivot Tables – Insert and Build

Introduction

First off, Excel writes pivot table as PivotTable, but I don't like that so I'm not going to do it. I did for the Excel 2019 books, but for this one I've decided not to. They let you search for pivot tables in the help screen just fine, so that's what we're going with.

Pivot tables are fantastic. I learned about them when I was in college and provided support to an Econ researcher who needed me to summarize some data. (He looked at me with horror when I confessed I didn't know what they were, but in my defense this was back in the day when I didn't even have a personal computer and the internet was not a place where I learned things.)

Once I learned about them, I was convinced that they are one of the most valuable tools in Excel. There is no better way to take a table of data and quickly summarize it.

In the beginner book and here I've occasionally used an anonymized version of one of my sales reports from Amazon. The one I'm using has 631 rows that include information for seven different author names with sales in ten different Amazon stores and three different sales types.

I could use filtering to see results for a single author, store, or transaction type. Or even combinations of those three. Or I could sort and then subtotal by one category. But pivot tables are just better. Let me show you.

Insert

Here are the first few rows of the data we're working with:

	A	B	C	D	E	F	G
1	Royalty Dat ˅	Author Name ˅	Marketplace ˅	Transaction Ty ˅	Net Units So ˅	Royalty ˅	Currency ˅
2	2021-01-31	Author A	Amazon.com	Standard	1	5.70	USD
3	2021-01-31	Author B	Amazon.com.au	Standard	1	5.03	AUD
4	2021-01-31	Author C	Amazon.com	Free - Price Match	65	0.00	USD
5	2021-01-31	Author D	Amazon.com	Standard	1	2.76	USD
6	2021-01-31	Author C	Amazon.fr	Free - Price Match	1	0.00	EUR
7	2021-01-31	Author C	Amazon.ca	Free - Price Match	3	0.00	CAD
8	2021-01-31	Author A	Amazon.com	Standard	1	5.83	USD
9	2021-01-31	Author C	Amazon.de	Free - Price Match	3	0.00	EUR

Because my worksheet is set up with the header information in the first row and then only rows of data after that, I can just select the whole worksheet. (Ctrl + A or click in the top left corner where that dark gray triangle is.)

You can work with data that starts elsewhere in your document, but what you do need to have is data that has a clear header row, no subtotals or grand totals, and ideally no breaks in columns or rows within the data. Also, no merged cells.

So get your data formatted properly and select it.

Next step is to go to the Insert tab and click on the image for PivotTable in the Tables section. Be sure to click on the image and not the dropdown arrow.

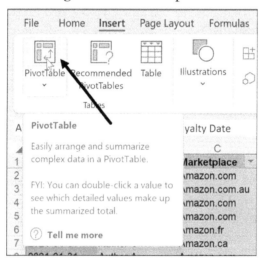

(The image is the same as the From Table/Range option in the dropdown, so if you click on the dropdown arrow accidentally (like I often do) you can just select that option.)

Your other choice there is to use an external data source, something we are not going to cover here. Working with external data increases the risk of something breaking along the way.

The PivotTable From Table Or Range dialogue box will appear.

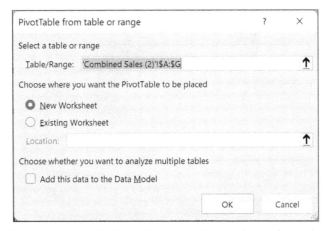

It will show your selected data and then give you the option of putting the table in a new worksheet or an existing worksheet.

I generally do not recommend putting a pivot table in the same worksheet as any other data so I almost always go with new worksheet.

I will on occasion put the pivot table in the same worksheet as my data when I know it's a one-off and that all of my data is already in place.

The reason not to put a pivot table in a worksheet with other data is because pivot tables are dynamic. They will change size and shape based upon what data is feeding into them.

So if I, for example, create a pivot table with author names in it and then add my own analysis text below that or to the right side, and later decide to add marketplace to the pivot table, I will have a problem. Because the pivot table will need to expand to include that new information but won't be able to because of my text. (Excel does at least tell you this is an issue before overwriting the text and gives you the chance to cancel doing so, but it's best to never have to worry about it in the first place.)

If you really do want that pivot table in your same worksheet as your data, then be sure to put it to the right or below any of your other data in that worksheet to avoid problems. Whatever cell you choose for placing the pivot table, Excel will build from that spot over and down.

Okay. So I'm leaving those settings alone because I already selected my data and want to put the table in a new worksheet, which means I can just click OK.

Excel will then open a new worksheet that has a blank pivot table in the main workspace and a PivotTable Fields task pane on the right-hand side.

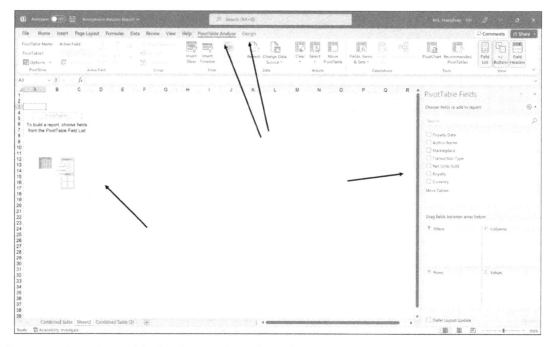

There are also PivotTable Analyze and Design tabs visible at the top of the workspace which we will cover in detail later. They will only be visible when you are working with the pivot table. Click on it to see them if you click away.

Build

You have two options for building your pivot table. You can check the boxes for the fields you want to include in your pivot table in the top of the task pane and let Excel place the fields for you where it thinks they make the most sense.

Or, and this is the method I use, you can place the fields yourself at the bottom of the task pane by left-clicking on each field name in the top section and dragging it down to one of the Filters, Columns, Rows, or Values boxes.

Here, for example, I have dragged Author Name into the Rows box and Net Units Sold into the Values box:

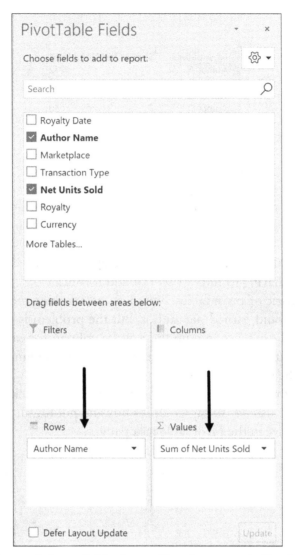

When I clicked and dragged those fields down, Excel automatically checked the box next to each field name in the top section.

That gives me a pivot table that has all of my author names listed on the left-hand side in rows and then, because I don't have anything in the Columns box, it leaves me with one single column next to that where the total number of units for each author is shown. Like so:

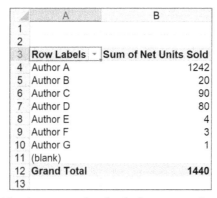

(Excel will automatically decide the type of calculation to perform on any field you put in the Values box. In this case, sum. But if you want to change that you can. We'll discuss how to do so later.)

So there we go. Less than a minute to summarize 600+ rows of data. And I can see all of it in one glance without having to filter or sort or add formulas.

That was the most basic of pivot tables. Now, let's start making more complex pivot tables.

I want to look at amount earned per author, but the problem is that this report includes different currencies, so I can't just sum up the Royalty column for each author because while maybe Euros and Dollars are about the same right now, something like Japanese Yen will throw everything out the window.

What I need is to list the amount earned in each currency for each author.

To do this, I can add Currency to my Columns box and put Royalty into the Values section.

This is what I now have in the pivot table task pane:

And this is what that pivot table looks like:

	A	B	C	D	E	F	G	H	I	J	K
1											
2											
3	Sum of Royalty	Column Labels									
4	Row Labels	AUD	CAD	EUR	GBP	INR	MXN	USD	(blank)	Grand Total	
5	Author A		12.35	108.12	13.03	337.01		40.25	5839.71		6350.47
6	Author B		15.09			28.42			22.79		66.3
7	Author C				0	0	0	0	8.98		8.98
8	Author D		3.79			7.43			293.38		304.6
9	Author E				2.56				14.71		17.27
10	Author F								0		0
11	Author G					0.35					0.35
12	(blank)										
13	Grand Total		31.23	108.12	15.59	373.21	0	40.25	6179.57		6747.97
14											

(We'll cover formatting later.)

Now let's build a pivot table that uses the Filter section to filter the entire pivot table based upon a field value. Here I've created a pivot table that has Author Name in Rows, Net Units Sold and Royalty in Values, and Transaction Type and Marketplace in Filters.

This is how that looks by default:

	A	B	C
1	Marketplace (All)		
2	Transaction Type (All)		
3			
4	**Row Labels**	**Sum of Net Units Sold**	**Sum of Royalty**
5	Author A	1242	6350.47
6	Author B	20	66.3
7	Author C	90	8.98
8	Author D	80	304.6
9	Author E	4	17.27
10	Author F	3	0
11	Author G	1	0.35
12	(blank)		
13	**Grand Total**	**1440**	**6747.97**
14			

But we put in filters for a reason, so let's go to the Transaction Type filter and click on the dropdown arrow:

I want to remove Free – Price Match from that list. To do so, I click on Select Multiple Items down there at the bottom of the dropdown. That's going to put checked boxes by each of the values up top and I can then uncheck Free – Price Match.

(If there are a lot of choices and you only want one, click the checkbox next to Select Multiple Items, and then click the box next to All to unselect all. You can then check the one or two you want. It's easier than unchecking each one individually.)

After you remove some of the values, that All in parens next to the field name will change to either Multiple Items or the one value you've chosen if you chose just one.

Here is that table with Marketplace limited to just one value, Amazon.com, and Transaction Type limited to all but Free – Price Match:

	A	B	C
1	Marketplace	Amazon.com	⊤
2	Transaction Type	(Multiple Items)	⊤
3			
4	**Row Labels**	**Sum of Net Units Sold**	**Sum of Royalty**
5	Author A	1129	5839.71
6	Author B	6	22.79
7	Author C	3	8.98
8	Author D	76	293.38
9	Author E	3	14.71
10	**Grand Total**	**1217**	**6179.57**
11			

To see which fields that Multiple Items is showing (or not showing), you can click on the filter symbol:

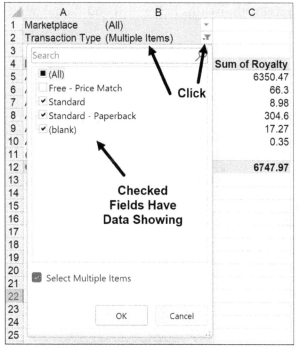

Now let's create an even more-complex pivot table that uses multiple fields for both Rows and Columns.

To do this, I went back to my original data table that's feeding this pivot table and added columns with month and year data and then refreshed the pivot table. (We'll cover Refresh later.)

For this new pivot table, I placed both year and month in Columns, both Author Name and Currency in Rows, and Royalty in Values:

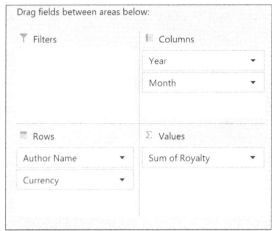

When you have more than one field in Columns or Rows, order matters. In this case I wanted Year to be the highest-level with months below that and then Author to be the highest level with currency below that.

Here's what that looks like:

	A	B	C	D	E	F	G	H	I	J	K	L	M
1													
2													
3													
4	Sum of Royalty	Column Labels											
5		2021				2021 Total	(blank)	(blank) Total	2020			2020 Total	Grand Total
6	Row Labels	January	February	March	April		(blank)		January	February	April		
7	Author A	350.56	342.83	3174.69	2091.06	5959.14			28.45	96.21	266.67	391.33	6350.47
8	AUD	9.96				9.96				2.39		2.39	12.35
9	CAD	27.14	5.75	47.49	23.85	104.23				3.89		3.89	108.12
10	EUR	1.66		4.2		5.86				7.17		7.17	13.03
11	GBP	15.44	30.68	188.53	84.74	319.39			4.85	8.5	4.27	17.62	337.01
12	MXN		40.25			40.25							40.25
13	USD	296.36	266.15	2934.47	1982.47	5479.45			23.6	74.26	262.4	360.26	5839.71
14	Author B	40.61	9.64	9.17		59.42				6.88		6.88	66.3
15	AUD	15.09				15.09							15.09
16	GBP	22.08	2.76	3.58		28.42							28.42
17	USD	3.44	6.88	5.59		15.91				6.88		6.88	22.79
18	Author C	8.98				8.98			0			0	8.98
19	CAD	0				0							0
20	EUR	0				0			0			0	0
21	GBP	0				0							0
22	INR	0				0							0
23	USD	8.98				8.98							8.98
24	Author D	22.43	54.64	128.46	68.3	273.83			8.63	8.28	13.86	30.77	304.6
25	AUD		3.79			3.79							3.79
26	GBP	0.35			7.08	7.43							7.43
27	USD	22.08	50.85	128.46	61.22	262.61			8.63	8.28	13.86	30.77	293.38
28	Author E	6.03		11.24		17.27							17.27
29	EUR	2.56				2.56							2.56
30	USD	3.47		11.24		14.71							14.71
31	Author F	0				0							0
32	USD	0				0							0
33	Author G	0.35				0.35							0.35
34	GBP	0.35				0.35							0.35
35	(blank)												
36	(blank)												
37	Grand Total	428.96	407.11	3323.56	2159.36	6318.99			37.08	111.37	280.53	428.98	6747.97

See that each author is listed first with their transactions broken down by currency and that each year of sales is listed first with the transactions by month listed under that.

It looks very complex but what it's showing is how much was earned each month of each year in each currency for each author.

By placing Author above Currency in the Rows section, the data is ordered with each currency listed for each author. If I had instead placed Currency first, it would be listed with each author for each currency. Like this:

	A	B	C	D	E	F
1						
2						
3						
4	Sum of Royalty	Column Labels				
5		2021				2021 Total
6	Row Labels	January	February	March	April	
7	AUD	25.05	3.79			28.84
8	Author A	9.96				9.96
9	Author B	15.09				15.09
10	Author D		3.79			3.79
11	CAD	27.14	5.75	47.49	23.85	104.23
12	Author A	27.14	5.75	47.49	23.85	104.23
13	Author C	0				0
14	EUR	4.22		4.2		8.42
15	Author A	1.66		4.2		5.86
16	Author C	0				0
17	Author E	2.56				2.56
18	GBP	38.22	33.44	192.11	91.82	355.59

See how now the data shows for each currency and then any author who had sales in that currency is listed below that?

Same thing happens in the Rows section.

I put year first and then month so that you have all monthly values listed under each year. If I'd reversed that order you'd have all yearly values listed under each month. So the table would start with January and then show both 2020 and 2021 values for January before then doing the same for February and then March.

Okay. So that's how to build pivot tables. Basically, make sure your data is formatted well for use with a pivot table, select it, insert a pivot table, and then click and drag the fields you want to use into place.

If you have more than one field in Rows or Columns, the order matters. The one listed first is the primary category.

You can put more than one field into the Values section, too, but I don't recommend doing so if the Columns and Rows sections are complex. Basically, step back when you're done and ask yourself if there's so much information in the table that it's too hard to follow. If there is, simplify and maybe use more than one pivot table. Or make some of those fields into filters. (Or add Slicers, which we'll discuss soon.)

Okay. That was the basics of how to insert and build pivot tables, but there's a lot more to this topic. Let's now cover some common tricks for working with a pivot table. Things I did in this chapter that I didn't want to stop to discuss at the time.

Pivot Tables – Work With

In the last chapter there were a number of basic tasks related to pivot tables that I performed but didn't cover or that I wanted to explain. They come up often enough that I wanted to highlight them in their own chapter. But later we'll more systematically go through the pivot table tabs and other options you have related to pivot tables to cover more obscure tasks, too.

So.

Change Calculation Type

We were very lucky in the last chapter that Excel recognized the value for Net Units Sold as a number that it could sum. Often with my data sets I receive from my vendors I am not that lucky. Excel brings in the numeric values in those workbooks as text and then defaults to *counting* the values instead of summing them up.

To fix this, click on the arrow on the right-hand side of the entry in the Values section, and choose Value Field Settings from the dropdown menu. Like here:

This will open the Value Field Settings dialogue box:

If you just want a basic calculation like sum or count it's available right there on the Summarize Values By tab.

You can make different choices for different columns of data if you have more than one field in the Values section. But be careful. Because it may not be immediately obvious that one column is a count, one is a sum of values, and one is an average.

I generally, unless my data labels and formats and other attributes make it abundantly clear, do not mix and match what I'm doing with multiple columns of data. Everything sums. Or everything takes the maximum value. Or everything takes the minimum value. Etc.

But it's a free world, you can do what you want. Just keep your audience in mind and make sure they'll quickly see what you've done.

There are two other ways to open the Value Field Settings dialogue box.

One is to click on an entry in your pivot table and go to the Active Field section of the PivotTable Analyze tab where you will see that field you selected listed. Click on Field Settings to open the Value Field Settings dialogue box and edit the settings for that field.

The other is to right-click on a value in the pivot table and then choose Value Field Settings from the bottom section of that dropdown menu.

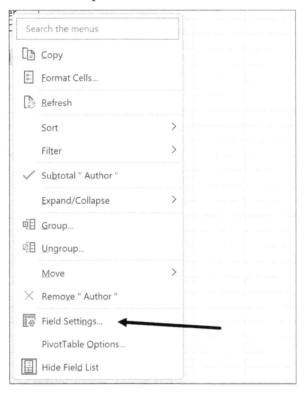

All of those options rely on using the Value Field Settings dialogue box. This is my general approach because at the same time I can format the cells.

But, that dropdown also lets you directly choose how to summarize values (sum, count, average, etc.) using the Summarize Values By option, which lists all of those choices in a dropdown menu format.

Use a Comparison Calculation

You can also do a comparison-style calculation with a field in your pivot table instead using the Show Values As tab in the Value Field Settings dialogue box or using the Show Values As dropdown menu:

As you can see, there are a large number of choices, such as % of Grand Total, % of Column Total, % of Row Total, and many many more.

You can actually add a field a second time and have one use of the field for a calculation like sum and the other use of the field for a comparison value like % of column total. I've done that here for Net Units Sold:

	A	B	C
1			
2			
3	Row Labels	Sum of Net Units Sold	Sum of Net Units Sold2
4	Author A	1242	86.25%
5	Author B	20	1.39%
6	Author C	90	6.25%
7	Author D	80	5.56%
8	Author E	4	0.28%
9	Author F	3	0.21%
10	Author G	1	0.07%
11	(blank)		0.00%
12	**Grand Total**	**1440**	**100.00%**

We can see that Author A is 86% of the units sold for the data set. Same as taking 1242, the actual total of the net units sold for Author A, and dividing by 1440, the total net units sold for all authors.

I can show both here and it looks fine because we're only looking at one variable, net units sold. If I were to add a second variable, like royalty, that would make things a bit messy, so I'd probably want to choose one or the other, but not display both. Again, think of your audience when building any pivot table or chart. Will they understand what they're seeing?

Remove a Field From a Pivot Table

The easiest way to remove a field from a pivot table is to just uncheck the checkbox in the top of the task pane. But if you used a field more than once like I did above and you want to remove only one of the uses, that won't work.

Another option is to click on the arrow to the right of the field name, and then click Remove Field from the dropdown.

Or you can right-click on one of the values for that field in the actual pivot table and choose the "Remove [X]" option from the dropdown menu, where X is the field name.

You can also left-click and drag the field away from the bottom of the task pane.

Sort Pivot Table Data

One of the things I often like to do when dealing with pivot tables is sort my data. I usually want my most successful authors or titles or series shown at the top of the table.

To sort a pivot table, right-click in a cell in the column where you want to sort, find Sort in the dropdown menu, and then choose the type of sort you want:

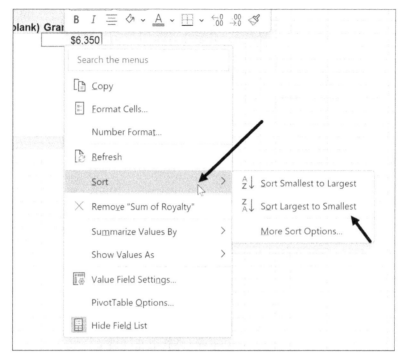

That will sort your data by the values in that selected column, in this case Column J, Grand Total:

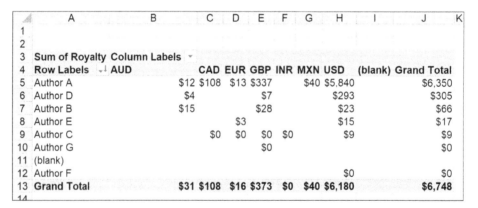

Now I have my largest values at the top and my smallest at the bottom.

Hide Entries in A Pivot Table

You can also hide certain entries by clicking on the arrow next to Row Labels or Column Labels and then unchecking the ones you don't want to see:

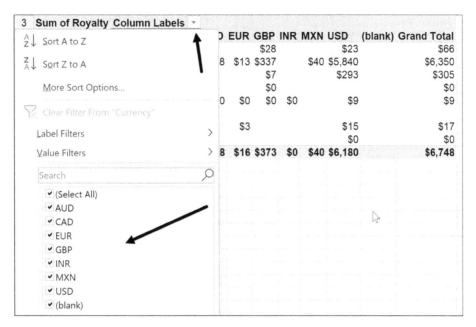

It works just like selecting or unselecting values when filtering data. I sometimes have "blank" as values in my tables and I don't need it there so I'll do this to remove it.

Here I made it so that only CAD transactions show:

	A	B	C
1			
2			
3	Sum of Royalty	Column Labels	
4	Row Labels	CAD	Grand Total
5	Author A	$108	$108
6	Author C	$0	$0
7	Grand Total	$108	$108
8			

Note that the arrow turned into a filter so you know that this is not a complete listing of all of your data.

Also, note how the pivot table size changed when I did that. There were only two authors with sales in Canada for that month, so not only did the number of columns go down, but so did the number of rows. Remember, pivot tables are dynamic, they adjust to display data based on your choices as to what to include or not include.

If there are two fields for columns or rows, click on a value in the pivot table for the one you want to edit first so that that's the dropdown menu that you see.

Group Values In a Row or Column in a Pivot Table

You can also group values in a row or column in a pivot table. Values you want to group *do not* have to be located next to each other. Select the values you want to group by clicking on the first one and then using Ctrl or Shift or clicking and dragging to select more.

Below I've chosen Authors C, E, and G, for example, by holding down Ctrl as I clicked on each one.

Once the values you want to group have been selected, right-click and choose Group from the dropdown menu:

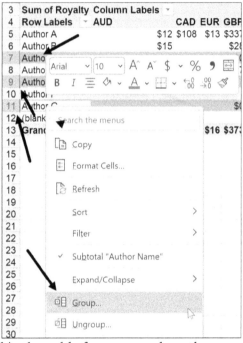

That will create a new level in that table for groups where the grouped values you selected are in one group and all other values are in their own group that only contains them and is named after them. Like so:

	Sum of Royalty Column Labels									
Row Labels	AUD	CAD	EUR	GBP	INR	MXN	USD	(blank)	Grand Total
Author A		$12	$108	$13	$337		$40	$5,840		$6,350
Author A		$12	$108	$13	$337		$40	$5,840		$6,350
Author B		$15			$28			$23		$66
Author B		$15			$28			$23		$66
Group1			$0	$3	$0	$0		$24		$27
Author C			$0	$0	$0	$0		$9		$9
Author E				$3				$15		$17
Author G					$0					$0
Author D		$4			$7			$293		$305
Author D		$4			$7			$293		$305
Author F								$0		$0
Author F								$0		$0
(blank)										
(blank)										
Grand Total		$31	$108	$16	$373	$0	$40	$6,180		$6,748

Group 1 contains Authors C, E, and G and then all of the other authors (and blank) have their own group.

The PivotTable Analyze tab also has a Group section where you can either group entries or ungroup them. You'll need to select your items first before you can use it.

Rename Group

When you click on a group name you should also see that name in your formula bar. You can edit the name by going to the formula bar and typing in what you want to use for that group:

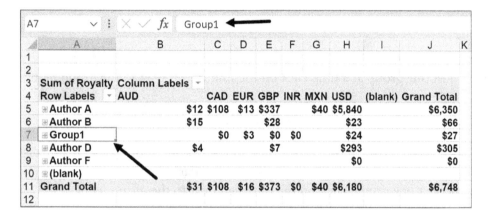

Collapse Groups

You can collapse the groups, like I have in the screenshot above, by right-clicking on a group name, going to Expand/Collapse in the dropdown menu, and choosing Collapse Entire Field.

		Search the menus		$337	$40	$5,840		$6,350
7	Author			$28		$23		$66
8	Autho	Copy		$28		$23		$66
9	Group1			$0	$0	$24		$27
10	Autho	Format Cells...		$0	$0	$9		$9
11	Autho					$15		$17
12	Autho	Refresh		$0				$0
13	Author			$7		$293		$305
14	Autho	Sort	>	$7		$293		$305
15	Author					$0		$0
16	Autho	Filter	>			$0		$0
17	(blank)							
18	(blank	✓ Subtotal "Author Name2"						
19	Grand To							$6,748
20		Expand/Collapse	>	+☰ Expand				
21		Group...		-☰ Collapse				
22								
23		Ungroup...		+☰ Expand Entire Field				

To collapse just one group at a time click on the minus sign next to the group name.

Expand Groups

To once again see the details for each group, right-click on a group name and then choose Expand Entire Field from the Expand/Collapse secondary dropdown.

To expand just one group, click on the plus sign next to the group name.

Clear Pivot Table

To start over, go to the Actions section of the PivotTable Analyze tab and use the Clear dropdown to select Clear All.

Remove Filters

If you have filters applied to your pivot table and you want to remove all of them, you can go to the Actions section of the PivotTable Analyze tab and choose Clear Filters from the Clear dropdown.

This will remove all filters from the pivot table, including the ones on your Column and Row Labels.

Refresh Pivot Table

If the data that is feeding into your pivot table changes, you need to refresh the pivot table.

To do so, go to the Data section of the PivotTable Analyze tab, and click on Refresh.

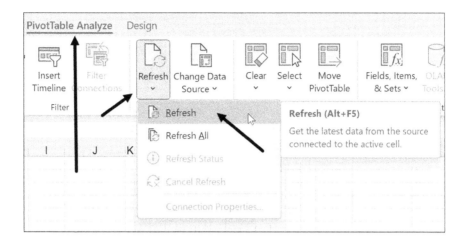

You can also use Alt + 5. (I just never remember it.)

The dropdown for Refresh has a Refresh All option which will refresh all data sources in the workbook. You can use this if you have multiple pivot tables that need refreshed.

If you change existing values in your data table or add new rows or columns into the middle of it, Refresh should work to update your pivot table or pivot table field choices.

But if you instead add data outside of the prior data range, then use the Change Data Source option right next to Refresh instead. That will bring up a dialogue box showing your current data selection. You can then change that range to include your new data.

* * *

Okay. So those are some basic common tasks I often need to perform with respect to pivot tables. Now let's talk about how to format your pivot table.

Pivot Tables – Format

In this chapter we're going to cover how to format your pivot table and the entries in that table. I'm going to start with a few formatting options that I use all the time and then we'll go through and be more systematic about your formatting options.

Value Field Settings Dialogue Box For Values Fields Formatting

As I mentioned above, I use the Value Field Settings Dialogue box to tell Excel what type of calculation to perform on my fields because it's also the best place to format the data in a pivot table.

You *can* just select fields in a pivot table and use the Home tab formatting options or right-click on selected fields and use the Number Format option in the dropdown menu. But the problem with those approaches is that they only apply formatting to those specific entries.

If you expand the data in your table at some point, the new entries will not be formatted that way. So if I start with just Author Name in my table and manually format those entries but then add Currency, all of the new entries will not be formatted.

But if you use the Value Field Settings Dialogue box to format the entries for that field, they will.

So how do you do this?

Open the Value Field Settings dialogue box and click on the option for Number Format in the bottom left corner.

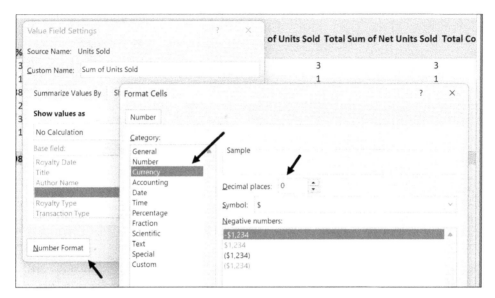

This will open the Format Cells dialogue box where you can then choose how to format the values in that field.

I usually need to do this for currency values to make them look like currency. I will often set the decimal places to zero when I do this to remove clutter from my table.

Subtotals and Grand Totals

Here is a standard complex pivot table that Excel will create by default:

Sum of Royalty	Column Labels											
	2021				2021 Total	(blank)	(blank) Total	2020			2020 Total	Grand Total
Row Labels	January	February	March	April		(blank)		January	February	April		
⊟ AUD	25.05	3.79			28.84				2.39		2.39	31.23
Author A	9.96				9.96				2.39		2.39	12.35
Author B	15.09				15.09							15.09
Author D		3.79			3.79							3.79
⊟ CAD	27.14	5.75	47.49	23.85	104.23				3.89		3.89	108.12
Author A	27.14	5.75	47.49	23.85	104.23				3.89		3.89	108.12
Author C	0				0							0
⊟ EUR	4.22		4.2		8.42			0	7.17		7.17	15.59
Author A	1.66		4.2		5.86				7.17		7.17	13.03
Author C	0				0			0			0	0
Author E	2.56				2.56							2.56
⊟ GBP	38.22	33.44	192.11	91.82	355.59			4.85	8.5	4.27	17.62	373.21
Author A	15.44	30.68	188.53	84.74	319.39			4.85	8.5	4.27	17.62	337.01
Author B	22.08	2.76	3.58		28.42							28.42
Author C					0							0
Author D	0.35			7.08	7.43							7.43
Author G	0.35				0.35							0.35
⊟ INR	0				0							0
Author C	0				0							0
⊟ MXN		40.25			40.25							40.25
Author A		40.25			40.25							40.25
⊟ USD	334.33	323.88	3079.76	2043.69	5781.66			32.23	89.42	276.26	397.91	6179.57
Author A	296.36	266.15	2934.47	1982.47	5479.45			23.6	74.26	262.4	360.26	5839.71
Author B	3.44	6.88	5.59		15.91				6.88		6.88	22.79
Author C	8.98				8.98							8.98
Author D	22.08	50.85	128.46	61.22	262.61			8.63	8.28	13.86	30.77	293.38
Author E	3.47		11.24		14.71							14.71
Author F	0				0							0
⊟ (blank)												
(blank)												
Grand Total	428.96	407.11	3323.56	2159.36	6318.99			37.08	111.37	280.53	428.98	6747.97

If you look across that top row you can see that Excel added subtotals for each year to the table. There's also a grand total row at the bottom.

I often generate pivot tables just to get data to work with, and when I do that I do not want all of that extraneous summary information, I just want the data. So I will often remove the subtotals and grand totals.

To edit your subtotals and grand totals, go to the Layout section of the pivot table Design tab.

The first option there is for Subtotals:

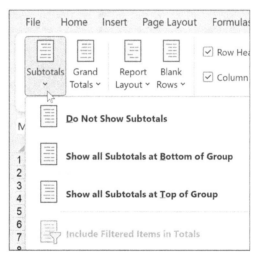

If you just want to remove your subtotals, then click on the Do Not Show Subtotals option.

The other two options you can see there let you decide where to display any subtotals for your rows. By default, at least with my settings, the subtotals show at the bottom of the group. Like here for Group 1:

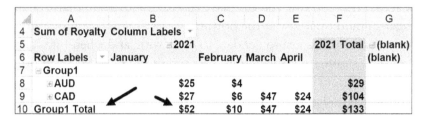

	A	B	C	D	E	F	G
4	Sum of Royalty	Column Labels ▾					
5		⊟2021				2021 Total	⊟(blank)
6	Row Labels ▾	January	February	March	April		(blank)
7	⊟Group1						
8	⊞AUD		$25	$4			$29
9	⊞CAD		$27	$6	$47	$24	$104
10	Group1 Total		$52	$10	$47	$24	$133

You can see the label for Group 1 and then the details for the group and then the Group 1 Total. But in this dropdown you can change that so that the subtotals show on the top instead. Like here where the subtotals for the group now show on the same row as the group name:

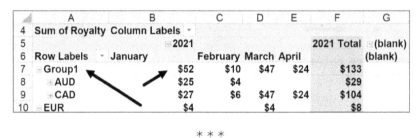

	A	B	C	D	E	F	G
4	Sum of Royalty	Column Labels ▾					
5		⊟2021				2021 Total	⊟(blank)
6	Row Labels ▾	January	February	March	April		(blank)
7	⊟Group1		$52	$10	$47	$24	$133
8	⊞AUD		$25	$4			$29
9	⊞CAD		$27	$6	$47	$24	$104
10	⊟EUR		$4		$4		$8

* * *

Next up is the Grand Totals dropdown:

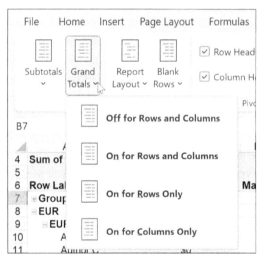

You can choose to have grand totals for rows only, columns only, both, or neither. If I plan on using the data in my pivot table for a chart (not a pivot chart, but just a basic chart), I will turn them all off. Because what I want is a header row with just data underneath.

Here is that same table from above but now with no subtotals or grand totals.

	A	B	C	D	E	F	G	H	I
4	Sum of Royalty	Column Labels ▾							
5		2021				(blank)	2020		
6	Row Labels ▾	January	February	March	April	(blank)	January	February	April
7	AUD								
8	Author A	$10						$2	
9	Author B	$15							
10	Author D		$4						
11	CAD								
12	Author A	$27	$6	$47	$24			$4	
13	Author C	$0							
14	EUR								
15	Author A	$2		$4				$7	
16	Author C	$0					$0		
17	Author E	$3							
18	GBP								
19	Author A	$15	$31	$189	$85		$5	$9	$4
20	Author B	$22	$3	$4					
21	Author C	$0							
22	Author D	$0			$7				
23	Author G	$0							
24	INR								
25	Author C	$0							
26	MXN								
27	Author A		$40						
28	USD								
29	Author A	$296	$266	$2,934	$1,982		$24	$74	$262
30	Author B	$3	$7	$6				$7	
31	Author C	$9							
32	Author D	$22	$51	$128	$61		$9	$8	$14
33	Author E	$3		$11					
34	Author F	$0							
35	(blank)								
36	(blank)								

Pivot Table Display Options

I can't use the pivot table in that image above as a data table. Right? If I copied and pasted it right now I'd have my values split across multiple rows. The currency for each entry isn't on the same line as the author name or results.

I can fix that though using the Report Layout dropdown menu:

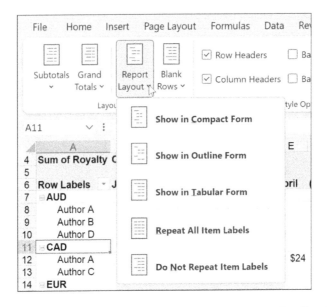

Your three main formatting options there are Compact Form, Outline Form, and Tabular Form. The thumbnail image next to each one tries to show what it would look like, but I often just apply them to see which one I want.

Below that you have the option to either Repeat All Item Labels or not.

If I'm trying to turn a pivot table into a data table, I choose Repeat All Item Labels and Tabular Form. That gives me this:

	A	B	C	D	E	F	G	H	I	J
4	Sum of Royalty		Year	Month						
5			2021	2021	2021	2021	(blank)	2020	2020	2020
6	Currency	Author Name	January	February	March	April	(blank)	January	February	April
7	AUD	Author A	$10						$2	
8	AUD	Author B	$15							
9	AUD	Author D		$4						
10	CAD	Author A	$27	$6	$47	$24			$4	
11	CAD	Author C	$0							
12	EUR	Author A	$2		$4				$7	
13	EUR	Author C	$0					$0		
14	EUR	Author E	$3							
15	GBP	Author A	$15	$31	$189	$85		$5	$9	$4
16	GBP	Author B	$22	$3	$4					
17	GBP	Author C	$0							
18	GBP	Author D	$0			$7				
19	GBP	Author G	$0							
20	INR	Author C	$0							
21	MXN	Author A		$40						
22	USD	Author A	$296	$266	$2,934	$1,982		$24	$74	$262
23	USD	Author B	$3	$7	$6				$7	
24	USD	Author C	$9							
25	USD	Author D	$22	$51	$128	$61		$9	$8	$14
26	USD	Author E	$3		$11					
27	USD	Author F	$0							
28	(blank)	(blank)								
29										

I can now select the whole worksheet, use Ctrl + C to copy and then Paste Special – Values to replace my pivot table with a data table. I will still have to change that top two rows of the table into one row that combines month and year data, but this gives me a summarized data table I can use to create an ordinary chart.

Here that is:

	A	B	C	D	E	F	G	H	I
2	Currency	Author Name	January-2021	February-2021	March-2021	April-2021	January-2020	February-2020	April-2020
3	AUD	Author A	9.96					2.39	
4	AUD	Author B	15.09						
5	AUD	Author D		3.79					
6	CAD	Author A	27.14	5.75	47.49	23.85		3.89	
7	CAD	Author C	0						
8	EUR	Author A	1.66		4.2			7.17	
9	EUR	Author C	0				0		
10	EUR	Author E	2.56						
11	GBP	Author A	15.44	30.68	188.53	84.74	4.85	8.5	4.27
12	GBP	Author B	22.08	2.76	3.58				

Note that there is a chapter on pivot charts later in this book if you don't want to do what I just did. Pivot charts let you build a chart directly from a pivot table. Which has the added benefit of remaining dynamic and adjusting as your data changes and you refresh your pivot table. Of course, that can also sometimes be a detriment. I often do that Paste Special – Values trick so that I lock in my values and don't inadvertently delete or change data that is flowing into my charts or calculations.

* * *

Okay. So those are the formatting options I use often with pivot tables in Excel. I format the entries in the Values section, I remove subtotals and grand totals, and I convert the table so that it can be copied and pasted-special and I have a good, working data table.

But there are many more formatting options than that. And it's time to walk through them.

Blank Rows

The final dropdown menu in the Layout section of the Design tab that we haven't covered yet is Blank Rows:

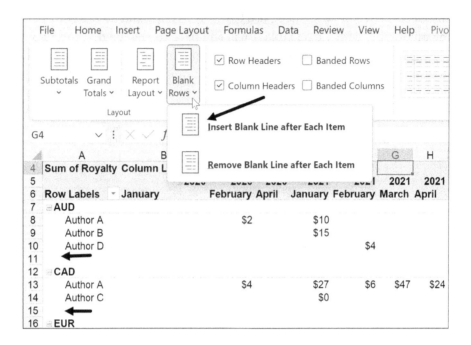

Blank Rows will let you insert a blank row after each "item". In this screenshot above an item is a group, so you can see blank rows that were inserted at Row 11 and Row 15.

I never use this one, but you might want to use it if you need a bit of visual separation between each of your top-level groups in your pivot table. It tends to break the visual of your data as you scan downward so that groups are more distinctive.

PivotTable Style Options and PivotTable Styles

Now let's look at the PivotTable Style Options and PivotTable Styles sections of the Design tab.

I'm going to skip to the styles first. I want to click on that down-pointing arrow with a line above it in the bottom right corner there as seen in the screenshot above. What that does is expands that section to show more styles:

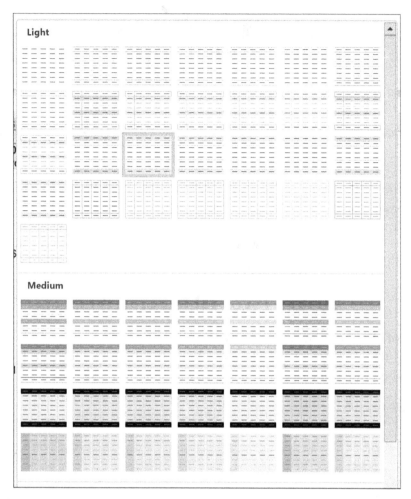

This will probably be a little hard to see in black and white print but essentially what you're seeing here are about sixty different pre-formatted pivot tables. Some have darker colored bands for the header row, some don't. Some use colored bands for subtotal rows, some don't. Some section off the first column, some don't.

There are a lot of choices. And if you scroll down you can see even more.

You can also see that the default style we've been working with so far is one of the choices in the Light section, in the third row. (As of December 2022.)

Hold your mouse over each style in the dropdown and Excel will show you in your worksheet what that style will look like. Click on the style to actually apply it.

Here I've applied Light Blue, Pivot Style Medium 6. (You can see the name when you hold your mouse over each option.)

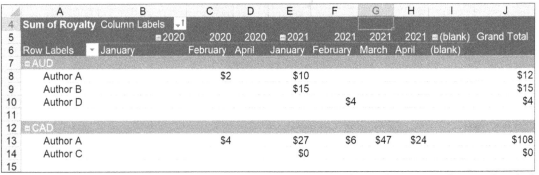

	Sum of Royalty	Column Labels								
		2020	2020	2020	2021	2021	2021	2021	(blank)	Grand Total
	Row Labels	January	February	April	January	February	March	April	(blank)	
	AUD									
	Author A		$2		$10					$12
	Author B				$15					$15
	Author D					$4				$4
	CAD									
	Author A		$4		$27	$6	$47	$24		$108
	Author C				$0					$0

It has a little more substance to it than the default style. Also, that extra formatting helps distinguish the values in the table.

Once you've applied a style, you can then use those checkboxes in the PivotTable Style Options section to add or remove row headers, column headers, banded rows, and banded columns formatting. The best way to see what it will do is just check and uncheck those boxes.

Custom Pivot Table Formatting

What if none of those options really give you what you want? Click on the New PivotTable Style option at the very bottom of the dropdown to bring up the New PivotTable Style dialogue box where you can customize everything to your heart's desire:

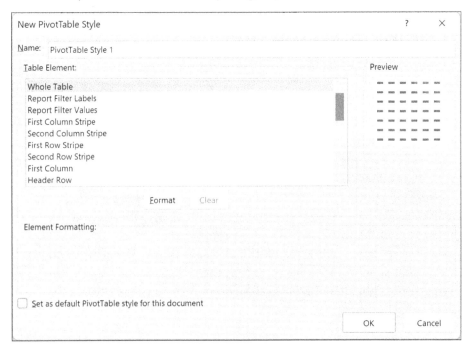

We are not going to go any further down that rabbit hole in this book. Suffice it to say it exists and if you really feel inspired it is there for you to use.

Pivot Tables – More Advanced Analysis

Okay, so I covered some very basic sorting, filtering, and grouping already which is where I spend 98% of my time when dealing with pivot tables, but there's more you can do.

So let's cover that part now. To do this, we need to go to the PivotTable Analyze tab and look at the Filter and Calculations sections.

Slicers

The first choice in the Filter section is Insert Slicer. Click on that and an Insert Slicers dialogue box will appear that lists all of your available fields.

Slicers will sit on top of your workspace and work much like the filter options, letting you pick and choose which values appear in your pivot table. Here I've chosen to show them for Month and Year:

Sum of Royalty	Column Labels								
	2020	2020	2020	2021	2021	2021	2021	(blank)	Grand Total
Row Labels	January	February	April	January	February	March	April	(blank)	
AUD									
Author A		$2		$10					$12
Author B				$15					$15
Author D					$4				$4
CAD									
Author A		$4		$27	$6	$47	$24		$108
Author C				$0					$0
EUR									
Author A		$7		$2		$4			$13
Author C	$0			$0					$0
Author E				$3					$3
GBP									
Author A	$5	$9	$4	$15	$31	$189	$85		$337
Author B				$22	$3	$4			$28
Author C				$0					$0
Author D				$0			$7		$7
Author G				$0					$0
INR									
Author C				$0					$0
MXN									
Author A					$40				$40
USD									
Author A	$24	$74	$262	$296	$266	$2,934	$1,982		$5,840
Author B		$7		$3	$7	$6			$23
Author C				$9					$9
Author D	$9	$8	$14	$22	$51	$128	$61		$293
Author E				$3		$11			$15
Author F				$0					$0

Year: 2020, 2021, (blank)

Month: January, February, March, April, (blank)

You can left-click and drag each box to move it, which I've done here to place the two slicers to the right-hand side of the pivot table.

Now that they're there I can click on those options to manipulate my pivot table. Here I've chosen to only display information for January 2020:

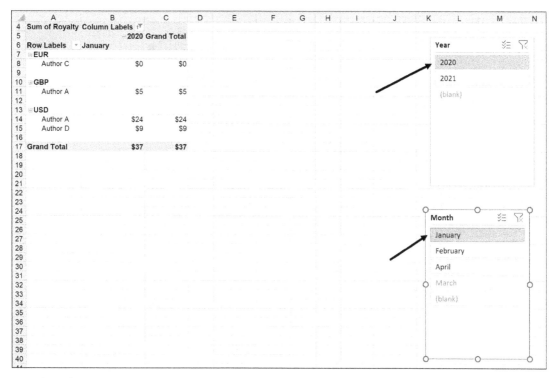

Note that the slicers stay where you've positioned them, but the pivot table, being dynamic, shrinks to only show my limited values. Keep this in mind if you feel tempted to move your slicers around when your pivot table is filtered, because as soon as I remove my filtering, that pivot table is going to go back to taking up that entire space once more.

To select January and 2020, I just clicked on them in each slicer.

But if you want to select more than one value in the slicer, you either need to use Alt + S or click on that icon with the checkmarks and lines next to them at the top of the slicer for that field. (See below. Alt + S basically turns that on.)

What you need to do at that point will depend on whether you've already selected a value or not. If all values are still selected, then as you click on a value it will be *unselected*. If you had already clicked on one value and then realized you wanted more than one, as you click on values they will be selected.

So pay attention to whether a field is shaded (like January and 2020 are in the last screenshot), or not. The shaded ones are the ones you're seeing results for.

To remove any applied filters from a slicer, use Alt + C or click on that little filter with an X on it in the top right corner of each filter. (Alt + C will only work if you select the filter first.)

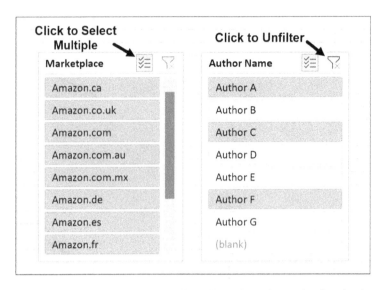

Another option is the Clear Filters option in the Clear dropdown in the Actions section of the PivotTable Analyze tab that we covered previously but remember that will remove all filters in your pivot table as well as all of your slicers.

Slicers remain visible even when you're not clicked onto the pivot table. The advantage to using them over putting a field into the Filters section is that when you have multiple values selected but not all values, you'll be able to see which ones. Also, it's much more intuitive for users to just click on what they can see as opposed to try to use dropdown menus.

Timeline

Next to the slicer is another option, Insert Timeline, which is specific to fields that are dates.

I find this one very tricky to work with, because it doesn't always recognize dates in my data as dates.

For example, I've been showing you anonymized data from an Amazon report. There is a Date field in that data, but when I used that field, Excel told me it was not a date field. Okay, fine. I went back to that data and formatted it as a date. Still not a date field according to Excel. Okay…I copied and pasted special values into a new worksheet and then formatted as a date. Still not a date according to Excel.

Next, I used the DATE function to build a date. Finally, that worked. Excel saw that as a date.

But…weirdly enough, when I added the Date field to my pivot table it would only display the dates in the table as their month. Even when I tried to change the format.

Good news, though. The Timeline option let me filter the data by day of the month, year, and quarter, so even though I couldn't get that information to display in the table itself, I could filter by it.

Here's that table with the timeline set to DAYS to show the days of the month I could filter by:

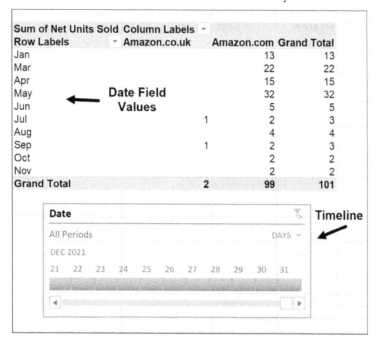

I can change the available choices in the timeline by using that dropdown there that currently says DAYS and setting it to YEARS, QUARTERS, or MONTHS.

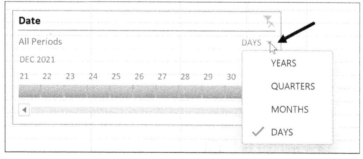

As that changes from DAYS to YEARS to QUARTERS to MONTHS, the available options also change to reflect that choice.

From what I can tell, the available choices will cover the date range from first date to last date, so especially with DAYS, even if there are no results on a particular day it will still show that date as an available option in the timeline if it's between the first and last dates in your data. For example, as you can see above in the pivot table there are not dates in December in this data, and yet the timeline shows December dates to choose from.

Click on any of those values to filter your table. Here I've changed it to YEARS and chosen 2021:

From what I can tell, it's not possible to choose date values that aren't connected, but you can click on one entry, hold down the Shift key and click on a later entry to select a date range, like I've done here for January 1 through 8, 2020:

Sum of Net Units Sold	Column Labels	
Row Labels	Amazon.com	Grand Total
Jan	13	13
Grand Total	**13**	**13**

Date		
Jan 1 - 8 2020		DAYS
JAN 2020		
1 2 3 4 5 6 7 8 9 10 11		

Note also that there is a scroll bar below the entries in the timeline so that if there are more available entries than you can see, you can scroll right or left to see the rest of them.

To remove a filter from your timeline, click on the funnel with the X in the top corner. Or use the Clear Filters option in the PivotTable Analyze tab.

Okay, that's the timeline. Don't feel bad if it doesn't work well for you, because it never does for me.

Format Your Slicer or Timeline

First, because we haven't covered this yet, to remove a slicer or a timeline, just click on it and then use the Delete key.

If you want to format your slicer or timeline, you can do so. When you insert a slicer or timeline there will be a menu tab up top that says Slicer or Timeline that has pre-formatted style choices as well as a new style option at the bottom of that list. Here is the one for the Slicer:

More interesting to me is the right-hand side of that tab for any slicer, because it includes a Buttons and Size section.

Size lets you specify the size of your slicer. Buttons lets you change the size of the options in the slicer or timeline and also display them in multiple columns, which can be very useful when there are a lot of potential values, like here where I've changed it to show the values in two columns instead of one:

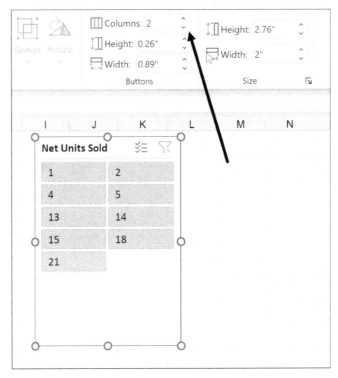

The timeline option does not allow that, it's very basic in terms of how it shows values. But you can at least change the size and the colors used if you want.

Calculated Fields

I will often want to take the values from a pivot table and do further analysis with them. Usually what I do is copy and paste that pivot table as special values, which gives me the data but keeps me from having to worry about the pivot table's dynamic nature which can move data around and is also very hard to reference from outside of the pivot table.

But my solution is not ideal, because sometimes you want to be able to look at your data over time and not have to rebuild your calculations every time. In that case, it's a good idea to build the calculations directly into the pivot table.

The way to do this is by using Calculated Fields. Let's walk through how to do that now.

Go to the Fields, Items, & Sets dropdown menu in the Calculations section of the PivotTable Analyze tab and choose Calculated Field.

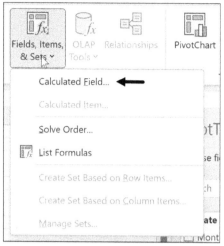

This will open the Insert Calculated Field dialogue box:

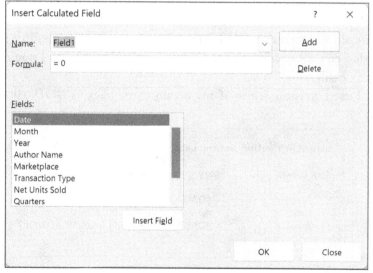

First step, name the field. I usually don't include spaces, so I'm going with RevPerUnit.

Next step is to build the formula. We're going to stick with simple math here. What I want is the Royalty field divided by the Net Units Sold field.

So I click into the formula field, delete the 0, go to the Fields section, find Royalty, double-click on it to insert (or click on it once and then click on Insert Field), type a / for division into the formula field and then go and do the same for Net Units Sold.

That gives me this:

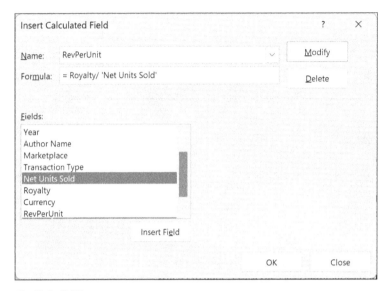

When I'm done, I click OK.

Excel automatically inserted the field into the Values section for me. But it's also now part of the list of fields I can choose from to insert into my pivot table, so I could use it as a filter, for example, just as easily.

Now, because I used division, some of my results came back as #DIV/0! results so it's not pretty right now:

	A	B	C	D	E
4	Sum of RevPerUnit	Column Labels			
5		2020	2020	2020	2021
6	Row Labels	January	February	April	January
7	AUD				
8	Author A	#DIV/0!		$2 #DIV/0!	$5
9	Author B	#DIV/0!	#DIV/0!	#DIV/0!	$5
10	Author D	#DIV/0!	#DIV/0!	#DIV/0!	#DIV/0!
11					
12	CAD				

But I can maybe modify that calculation. How to do so is not intuitive. What you do is go back to that dropdown and choose Calculated Field again and then for the Field Name you type in the exact same name as before. That will change your option for that field from Add to Modify. Type in the new formula you want, click on Modify, and then OK.

The formula I was able to get to work for this was:

$$=IF(ISERROR(Royalty\ /'Net\ Units\ Sold'),0,Royalty\ /'Net\ Units\ Sold')$$

It wasn't exactly what I wanted because I'd rather display a blank space than a zero value, but at least it got rid of those error messages.

	A	B	C	D	E
4	Sum of RevPerUnit	Column Labels			
5		2020	2020	2020	2021
6	Row Labels	January	February	April	January
7	AUD				
8	Author A		$0	$2	$0	$5
9	Author B		$0	$0	$0	$5
10	Author D		$0	$0	$0	$0
11					

(I know we haven't covered a lot of functions yet, but if you're curious about what I used there it was a combination of the IF function and the ISERROR function. Both are covered in the next book in this series or you can look them up in Excel's help.)

And, one more tip on this, if you ever need to see the formula you used for a calculated field, choose the List Formulas option. That's going to show you a new worksheet with all of your formulas in the order that they calculate.

It also has the added benefit of showing each formula so you can copy it if you need to make a small edit and don't want to try to recreate it from scratch. (I was unable to edit the formula directly on that worksheet, which would've been nice, but does not seem to be possible, at least not with fields that have spaces in their name.)

In general, I would recommend keeping your calculations simple in your pivot table, but again, you do you. If you can make it work, good on ya.

Conditional Formatting

While we're here talking about more advanced analysis, let's dip a toe in on applying conditional formatting to our pivot table entries. This is not something I have done a lot of in the past so I can't tell you how it will go wrong. But I can tell you how to do it.

Create your pivot table, select the cells that are in the main body of the pivot table, and then apply your conditional formatting like you would to any other cells.

I recommend that after you do that you go to Manage Rules and choose to edit the rule you just created. When you do so there will be an additional choice you can make:

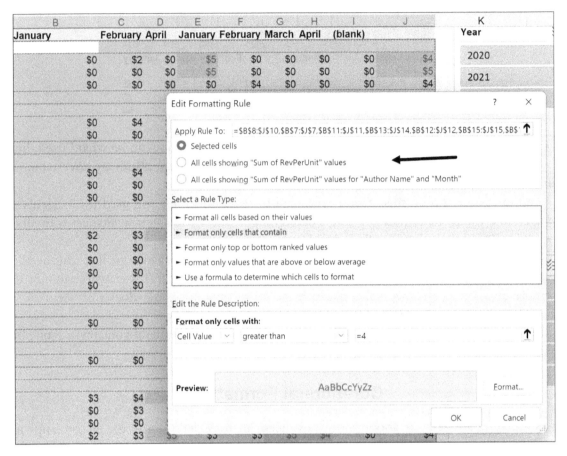

Right now if you look at the Apply Rule field you can see that Excel is using my selected data range. But I can check the box below that, which currently says "All Cells Showing Sum of RevPerUnit Values", to have it apply the rule to my field instead of those specific cells.

That way if the table updates I won't lose the conditional formatting for that field.

If I want to make sure the conditional formatting isn't lost, but also want to limit it to this specific combination that exists, I can check that last box which currently says, "All Cells Showing Sum of RevPerUnit Values for Author Name and Month". That way, if I use the RevPerUnit field in some other part of the pivot table it won't bring that conditional formatting with it.

Here I was able to add separate conditional formatting to two fields (Sum of Net Units Sold and Sum of Royalty) that I had in a pivot table:

	A	B	C
1			
2			
3			
4		Column Labels	
5		2021	2021
6		January	January
7	Row Labels	Sum of Net Units Sold	Sum of Royalty
8	USD	194	334.33
9			
10	GBP	16	38.22
11			
12	CAD	8	27.14
13			
14	AUD	5	25.05
15			
16	EUR	3	4.22

The trick was, or at least the way I got it to work, was to click into one cell in each column, add conditional formatting, and then edit the rule to expand it to all of that field not just that one cell.

It did take a little fiddling, so if it doesn't work the first time, don't give up. Alright, now let's talk for a moment about Pivot Charts.

Pivot Tables – Pivot Charts

Pivot charts did not always exist, so my default still tends to be old-school charts that I've been using for decades. But I've been experimenting enough with these that I feel comfortable mentioning this possibility to you.

What are pivot charts? They are the ability to create a chart straight from the data in a pivot table.

Here I have a very basic pivot table:

	A	B	C	D	E	F
1						
2	Currency	USD ▼				
3						
4	**Sum of Royalty**	**Column Labels** ▼				
5		≡**2021**	**2021**	**2021**	**2021**	**Grand Total**
6	**Row Labels** ▼	**January**	**February**	**March**	**April**	
7	Author A	296.36	266.15	2934.47	1982.47	5479.45
8	Author D	22.08	50.85	128.46	61.22	262.61
9	Author B	3.44	6.88	5.59		15.91
10	Author E	3.47		11.24		14.71
11	Author C	8.98				8.98
12	Author F	0				0
13	**Grand Total**	**334.33**	**323.88**	**3079.76**	**2043.69**	**5781.66**
14						

It shows four months of data for six authors for one currency. This type of data lends itself well to a column or bar chart, so let's try to create one of those using the PivotChart option located in the Tools section of the PivotTable Analyze tab.

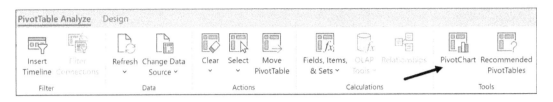

Click on PivotChart and it will bring up the familiar Insert Chart dialogue box:

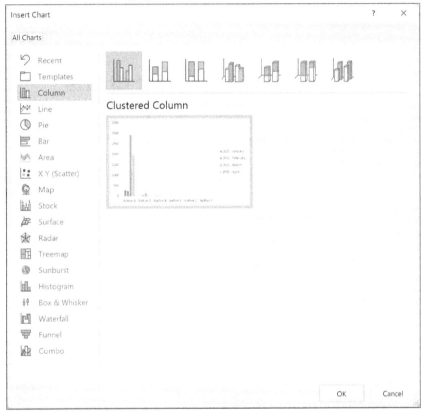

What I usually find at this point is that my pivot table is not set up the way that I want it to be for that particular chart. I don't know if you can see that here, but the Clustered Column chart it's showing has the four months for each author clustered together. But what I really want is all of the authors clustered together for each month.

I have two options here:

First, I could go back and fix my pivot table by swapping Author Name and Year and Month so that Year and Month are in the Rows section and Author Name is in the Columns section. If I want to do that, I click Cancel.

Second, I can go ahead and create the chart as-is and then fix it from there. I usually choose to fix it from there. So I click OK to go ahead and create my chart.

Once the chart is created, I can go to the Design tab and choose Switch Row/Column, which will fix the chart. *It will also change your pivot table* as you can see here:

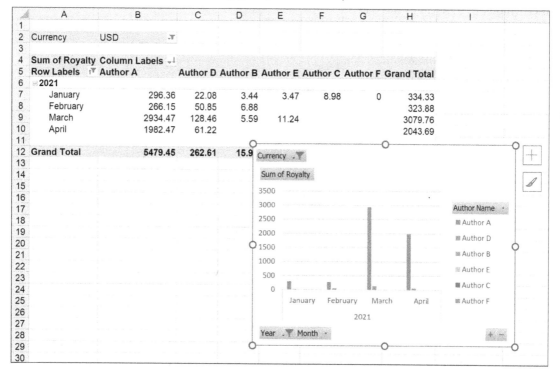

	A	B	C	D	E	F	G	H	I
1									
2	Currency	USD							
3									
4	Sum of Royalty	Column Labels							
5	Row Labels	Author A		Author D	Author B	Author E	Author C	Author F	Grand Total
6	2021								
7	January	296.36		22.08	3.44	3.47	8.98	0	334.33
8	February	266.15		50.85	6.88				323.88
9	March	2934.47		128.46	5.59	11.24			3079.76
10	April	1982.47		61.22					2043.69
11									
12	Grand Total	5479.45		262.61	15.9				

Looking at that chart, one author sort of drowns out everyone else so maybe a stacked column chart would be a better choice. At this point making that change is just like working with any other chart. I go to the Design tab, choose Change Chart Type, and then select my new chart type. Better.

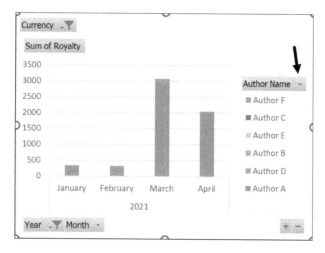

Or maybe I just don't need that author in the chart. If I click on the arrow next to Author Name (see the screenshot above) that will bring up a dropdown menu that lets me choose which values to include in the chart.

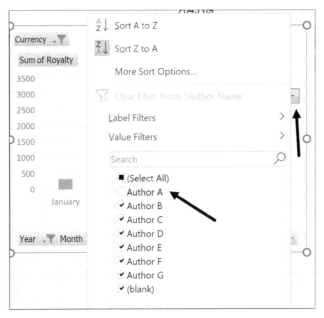

Above you can see that I unchecked Author A. Each field that's being used in the pivot table is available to select or not select. You can also use search, value filters, and label filters.

Here is the updated chart which shows far more detail for all of the other authors now:

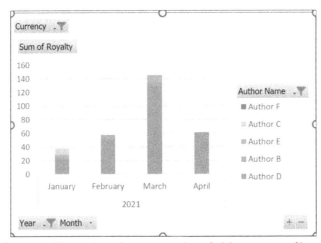

If you look at that chart you'll see that there are other fields you can filter directly on the chart such as Currency, Year, and Month.

Any changes you make to those filters will also be reflected in your pivot table. And vice versa. You can't change one without changing the other. You can, however, create a pivot chart, copy it, and then paste it as a picture to keep that chart you created without having it be impacted by future changes to the pivot table.

The same Chart Styles and formatting options exist for pivot charts as do for regular charts through the Design and Format tabs available up top when you click on your chart.

I find pivot charts to be more interactive than standard charts because of the ability to filter. So if I want to look at say, trend in sales over time for different authors or different series where I have too much data for one chart, rather than create six separate data tables and the charts to go with them, I can create one pivot chart and then quickly cycle through a subset of my data by using that filtering ability.

Just remember that your pivot chart is tied to your pivot table until you lock it in place as a picture. If the chart is being used for some sort of board reporting or regulatory reporting or something where it matters that it be fixed in time, do not leave it as a pivot chart. Lock it down. And, honestly, I'd lock down the data, too, but that's just me.

Okay. A few clean-up items and then we'll finally be done with pivot tables.

Pivot Tables – A Few More Items

Just a little bit of housekeeping before we wrap up this very extensive topic.

Move Pivot Table Values

You can move pivot table values around. So, for example, in my pivot table with Authors A, B, C, D, E, and F maybe I want authors A and E next to each other because they're the same genre.

To move a pivot table value, right-click on it and use the Move secondary dropdown menu to move the field to the beginning, up one, down one, or to the end. You can also use this option to move the field from columns to rows or from rows to columns.

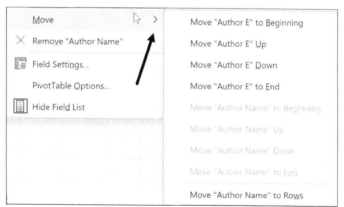

Name A Pivot Table

In the PivotTable Analyze tab there is a section on the left-hand side called PivotTable. You can name your pivot table there if you want to. I never have, but I do believe there are some advanced-level tasks in Excel that are easier if you name your pivot tables.

PivotTable Options

That same section also has an Options dropdown where you can click on Options to open a PivotTable Options dialogue box which contains a number of settings for that specific pivot table:

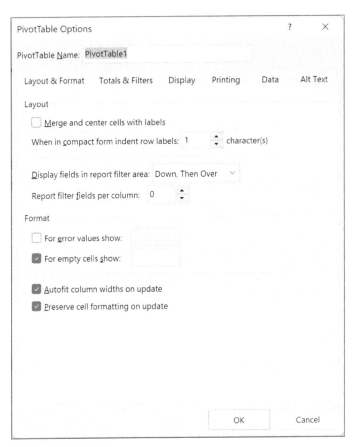

On the Totals & Filters tab you can turn off showing grand totals. On the Display tab you can choose the default sort order for data in your pivot table. On the Printing tab you can set print titles to select what prints at the top of each page or left-hand side of each page. On the Data tab you can set the pivot table to refresh each time you open the Excel file. And more. If you're curious, it's worth clicking through.

PivotTable Options is also available by right-clicking on the pivot table and choosing PivotTable Options from the dropdown menu.

Move PivotTable

In the Actions section of the PivotTable Analyze tab there is an option to move your pivot table. Click on that and you can either move the pivot table to a different location in an existing worksheet or to a new worksheet. Choose the new location based upon where the top left corner of the table will be. It doesn't take into account any filter fields you may have above that.

Recommended PivotTables

If you're not sure what pivot table you want to build or how to build one, there is a Recommended PivotTables option in the Tools section of the PivotTable Analyze tab. Click on that and it will take the data you selected for your pivot table and suggest various pivot tables:

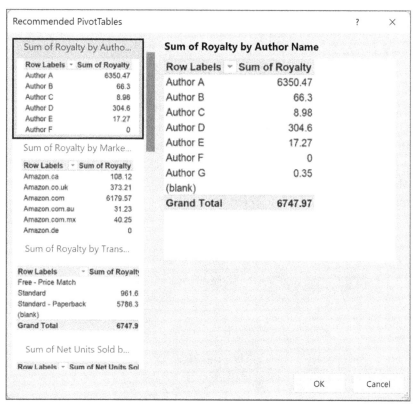

For basic pivot tables the suggestions are solid, but in my case they were all one by one tables. Also, the suggestions covered basically any numeric field combined with any text field which meant that towards the bottom it suggested combinations that made no sense.

But it does at least show you how a basic pivot table is built.

Show Options

At the very end of the PivotTable Analyze tab there are three options in the Show section. Field List turns on and off the PivotTable Fields task pane. Buttons hides or shows the expand/collapse buttons for grouped data or when you have multiple data levels. Field Headers hides or shows the Column Labels and Rows Labels text in the pivot table.

Linking Pivot Tables

It is beyond the scope of this book but Excel has in recent years been upgraded to allow for the linking of various data tables, which can create a data structure akin to what you do in Access or other database tools. That includes pivot tables.

If you want to explore that more, search for help on "work with relationships in PivotTables". It's not an area I've explored enough to give help.

Blank Entries

You may have noticed that some of the example pivot tables I showed you had a "blank" field value as well as the expected values. For me this usually occurs because I just selected the entire worksheet rather than a defined area that only had data in it. I usually just hide those entries or ignore them, but if they bother you the solution is usually going to be to be more careful in what data you select before choosing to insert a pivot table. Either that or to delete blank columns or rows from within your selected data.

Appendix A: Basic Terminology

These terms are defined in detail in *Excel 365 for Beginners*. This is just a quick overview in case it's needed.

Workbook

A workbook is what Excel likes to call an Excel file.

Worksheet

Excel defines a worksheet as the primary document you use in Excel to store and work with your data. A worksheet is organized into Columns and Rows that form Cells. A workbook can contain multiple worksheets.

Columns

Excel uses columns and rows to display information. Columns run across the top of the worksheet and, unless you've done something funky with your settings, are identified using letters of the alphabet.

The first column in a worksheet will always be Column A. And the number of columns in your worksheet will remain the same, regardless of how many columns you delete, add, or move around. Think of columns as location information that is actually separate from the data in the worksheet.

Rows

Rows run down the side of each worksheet and are numbered starting at 1 and up to a very high number. Row numbers are also locational information. The first row will always be numbered 1, the second row will always be numbered 2, and so on and so forth. There will also always be a fixed number of rows in each worksheet regardless of how many rows of data you delete, add, or move around.

Cells

Cells are where the row and column data comes together. Cells are identified using the letter for the column and the number for the row that intersect to form that cell. For example, Cell A1 is the cell that is in the first column and first row of the worksheet.

Click

If I tell you to click on something, that means to use your mouse (or trackpad) to move the cursor on the screen over to a specific location and left-click or right-click on the option. If you left-click, this selects the item. If you right-click, this generally displays a dropdown list of options to choose from. If I don't tell you which to do, left- or right-click, then left-click.

Left-click/Right-click

If you look at your mouse you generally have two flat buttons to press. One is on the left side, one is on the right. If I say left-click that means to press down on the button on the left. If I say right-click that means press down on the button on the right.

Select

If I tell you to "select" cells, that means to highlight them. You can either left-click and drag to select a range of cells or hold down the Ctrl key as you click on individual cells. To select an entire column, click on the letter for the column. To select an entire row, click on the number for the row.

Data

Data is the information you enter into your worksheet.

Data Table

I may also sometimes refer to a data table or table of data. This is just a combination of cells that contain data in them.

Arrow

If I tell you to arrow to somewhere or to arrow right, left, up, or down, this just means use the arrow keys to navigate to a new cell.

Cursor Functions

The cursor is what moves around when you move your mouse or use the trackpad. In Excel the cursor changes its appearance depending on what functions you can perform.

Tab

I am going to talk a lot about Tabs, which are the options you have to choose from at the top of the workspace. The default tab names are File, Home, Insert, Page Layout, Formulas, Data, Review, View, and Help. But there are certain times when additional tabs will appear, for example, when you create a pivot table or a chart.

(This should not be confused with the Tab key which can be used to move across cells.)

Dropdown Menus

A dropdown menu is a listing of available choices that you can see when you right-click in certain places such as the main workspace or on a worksheet name. You will also see them when you click on an arrow next to or below an option in the top menu.

Dialogue Boxes

Dialogue boxes are pop-up boxes that contain additional choices.

Scroll Bars

When you have more information than will show in a screen, dialogue box, or dropdown menu, you will see scroll bars on the right side or bottom that allow you to navigate to see the rest of the information.

Formula Bar

The formula bar is the long white bar at the top of the main workspace directly below the top menu options that lets you see the actual contents of a cell, not just the displayed value.

Cell Notation

Cells are referred to by their column and row position. So Cell A1 is the cell that's the intersection of the first column and first row in the worksheet.

When written in Excel you just use A1, you do not need to include the word cell. A colon (:) can be used to reference a range of cells. A comma (,) can be used to separate cell references.

When in doubt about how to define a cell range, click into a cell, type =, and then go and select the cells you want to reference. Excel will describe your selection in the formula bar using cell notation.

Paste Special Values

Paste Special Values is a way of pasting copied values that keeps the calculation results or the cell values but removes any formulas or formatting.

Task Pane

On occasion Excel will open a task pane, which is different from a dialogue box because it is part of the workspace. These will normally appear on the right-hand side in Excel for tasks such as working with pivot tables or charts or using the built-in Help function. (They often appear on the left-hand side in Word.)

They can be closed by clicking on the X in the top right corner.

About the Author

M.L. Humphrey is a former stockbroker with a degree in Economics from Stanford and an MBA from Wharton who has spent close to twenty years as a regulator and consultant in the financial services industry.

You can reach M.L. at mlhumphreywriter@gmail.com or at mlhumphrey.com.

* * *

If you want to learn more about Microsoft Excel, check out *Excel Tips and Tricks* or one of the main Excel 365 Essentials titles, *Excel 365 for Beginners*, *Intermediate Excel 365*, or *102 Useful Excel 365 Functions*.